Ho
Make and Use an Abax

By Amy Houts

CELEBRATION PRESS
Pearson Learning Group

Contents

The Abax and the Abacus

You don't have to use a pencil and paper to do math. You can use an **abax** (AB-aks). An abax is a **counting board**. It was created in Egypt thousands of years ago. An abax was a flat **frame** filled with sand. Lines were drawn in the sand, and pebbles were placed between the lines. People used the abax to do simple math.

The word *abax* comes from several old languages. In Greek, it means "a table sprinkled with sand and dust." In Hebrew, it means "dust." We don't know what the early Egyptians called their counting board, but *abax* is a good word to describe the tool.

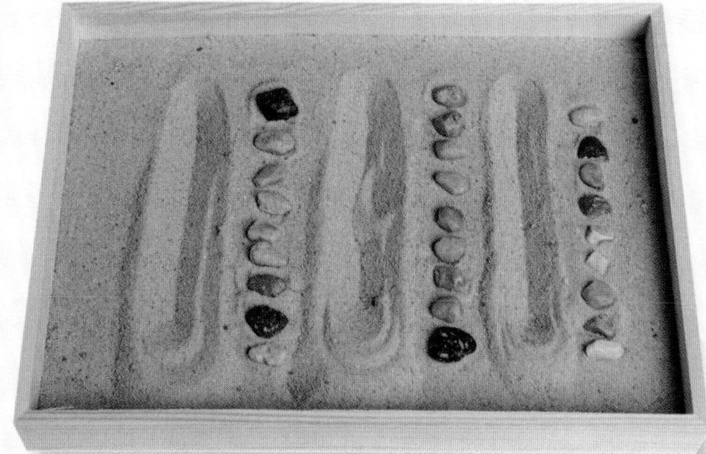

An abax might have looked like this counting board.

a Chinese abacus

a Russian abacus

To do harder math, the **abacus** (AB-uh-kuhs) was invented. The abacus is a frame with beads strung on rods. The beads can show very large numbers.

Many ancient cultures invented their own abacuses. For example, a type of abacus made of marble was used in Babylonia more than 2,000 years ago. Other types of abacuses were also used in ancient Rome, China, and Russia. Today, there are people around the world who use abacuses.

Both an abax and an abacus are different from calculators used today. Calculators do the math and show the answer. People who used an abax or abacus did much of the math in their heads. They used the abax or abacus to help them find the answers.

For example, to add numbers using **regrouping** on an abax, a person might have regrouped 10 ones into 1 ten in his or her head. Then that person would move the pebbles in the abax to show the addition and find the answer.

While an abax can't do everything a calculator can, it can help us do simple addition and subtraction. Read on to learn how to make and use your own abax.

A calculator is an easy tool to use.

How to Make an Abax

You can make an abax. Then you can use your abax to do math.

What You Need:

- air-dry clay
- a ruler
- a rolling pin
- a pencil
- 27 dried beans
- a plastic sandwich bag

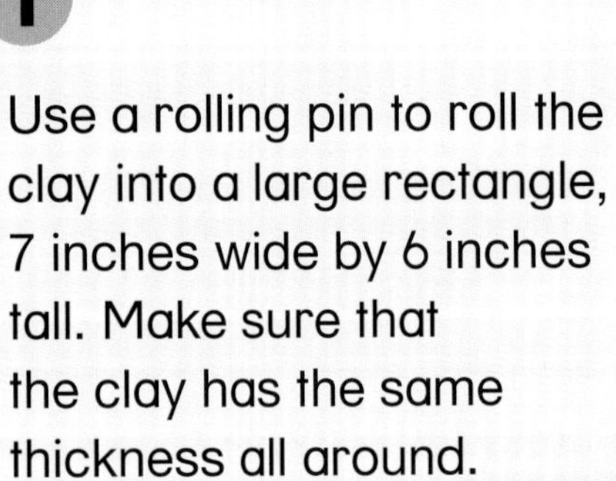

1

Use a rolling pin to roll the clay into a large rectangle, 7 inches wide by 6 inches tall. Make sure that the clay has the same thickness all around.

Measure your rectangle. Make sure that it is 7 inches wide by 6 inches tall. If you need to make your rectangle bigger, keep rolling.

3

Press the edge of the ruler down against the edges of the clay to make them straight. Remove the extra pieces of clay.

Now, use a pencil to make three **grooves**, or long narrow dents, in the clay. Make a groove near the right edge of the rectangle. Make a second groove in the middle of the rectangle. Make the last groove near the left edge of the rectangle.

Be careful: Do not make the grooves too deep. They might break through the clay.

5

Next, place 9 beans in each groove. Do they fit? If not, use the pencil to make the grooves longer. If the grooves are too long, pinch the clay together so that exactly 9 beans fit.

Important:

Only 9 beans should fit into each groove.

Remove the beans and place them in the bag. Wash your hands.

Allow your abax to dry overnight.

Caution:
If you plan to use the rolling pin to prepare food, wash it well with soap and water.

How to Use Your Abax

Now you can use your abax. An abax is an easy tool to use to do addition and subtraction. The grooves hold the beans. The beans are the **counters**. They are called *counters* because you use them to count.

When using an abax, you group numbers by ones, tens, and hundreds. You count ones in the groove on the right. You count tens in the groove in the middle. You count hundreds in the groove on the left.

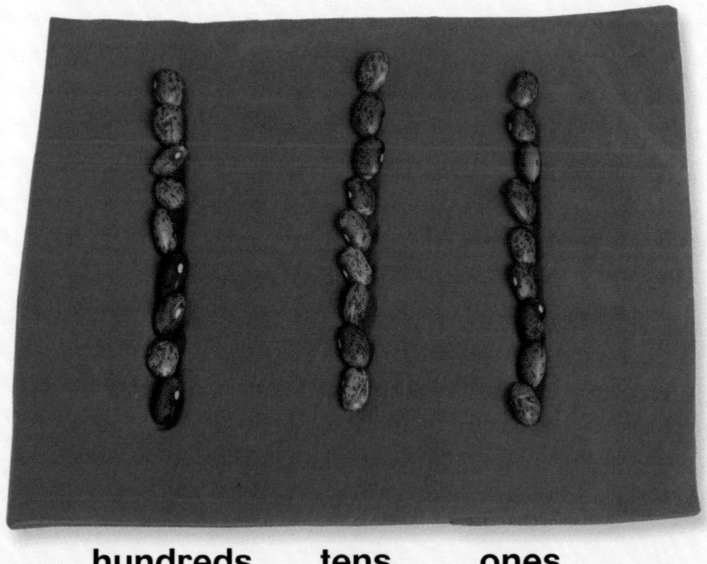

hundreds **tens** **ones**

Ones, Tens, and Hundreds

To show ones, you place counters in the ones groove. One counter shows the number 1. Four counters show the number 4, and so on. No counters in the abax show the number 0.

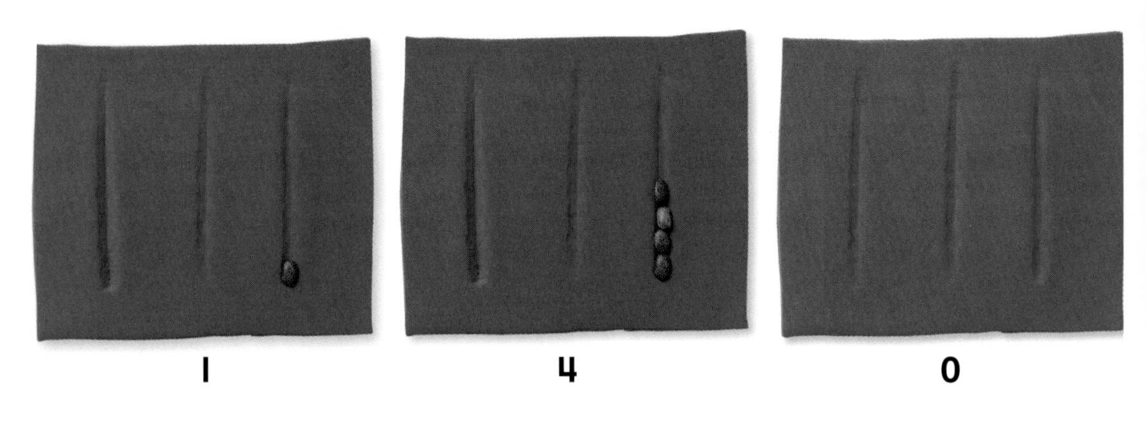

To show tens, you place counters in the tens groove. To show hundreds, you place counters in the hundreds groove.

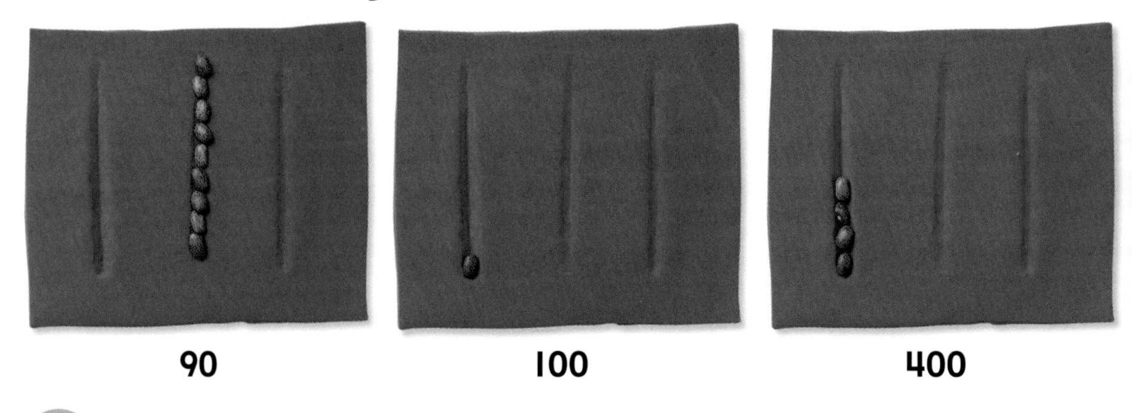

There are a few rules to remember:

- When placing counters into a groove, start at the bottom of the groove and work your way up.
- Only nine counters can fit into a groove.
- If all three grooves are completely filled, the abax shows the number 999. This number is the highest one that can be shown on an abax.

To show the number 42, place counters at the bottom of each groove.

A completely filled abax shows the number 999.

Adding With an Abax

Adding 13 and 15

Adding using an abax is easy. To add 13 and 15, first place counters in the abax to show the number 13. Place 3 counters in the ones groove and 1 counter in the tens groove. To add 15, place 5 more counters in the ones groove and another counter in the tens groove. You now have the number 28.

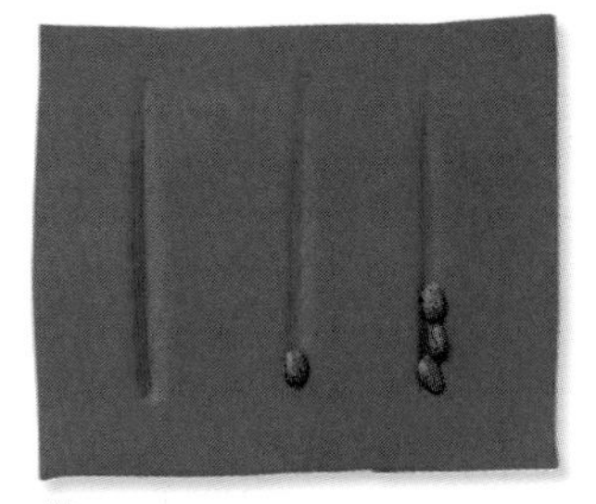

1 Show 13.

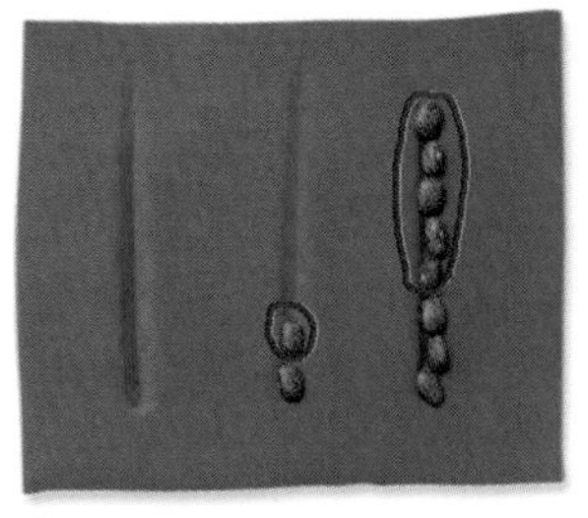

2 To add 15, put 5 counters in the ones groove and 1 counter in the tens groove.

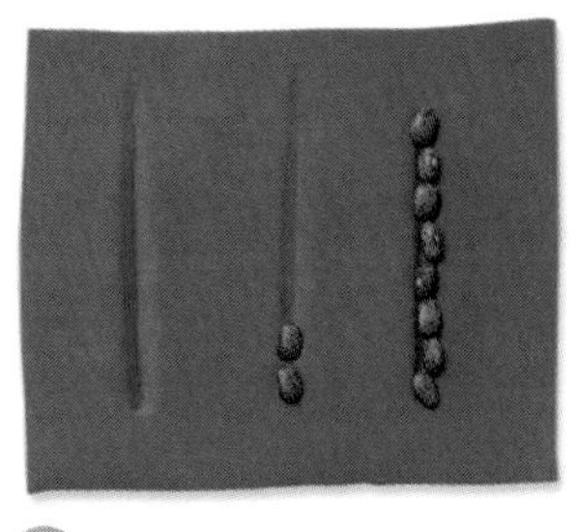

3 The sum is 28.

Subtracting With an Abax

Subtracting 16 from 19

To subtract 16 from 19, place counters in the abax to show the number 19. Place 9 counters in the ones groove and 1 counter in the tens groove. To subtract 16, remove 6 counters from the ones groove and the counter from the tens groove. You now have the number 3.

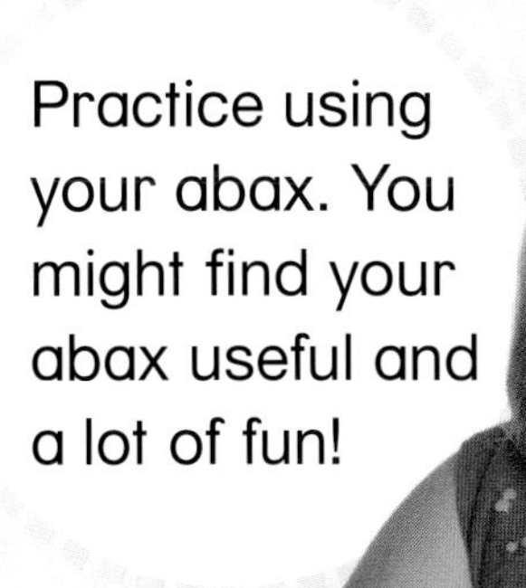

Practice using your abax. You might find your abax useful and a lot of fun!

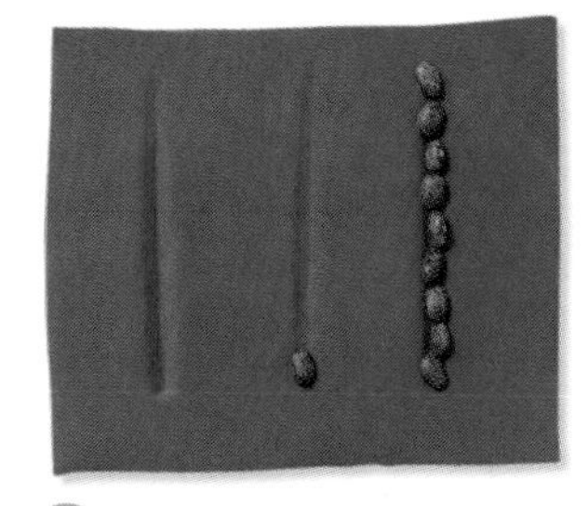

1 Show 19.

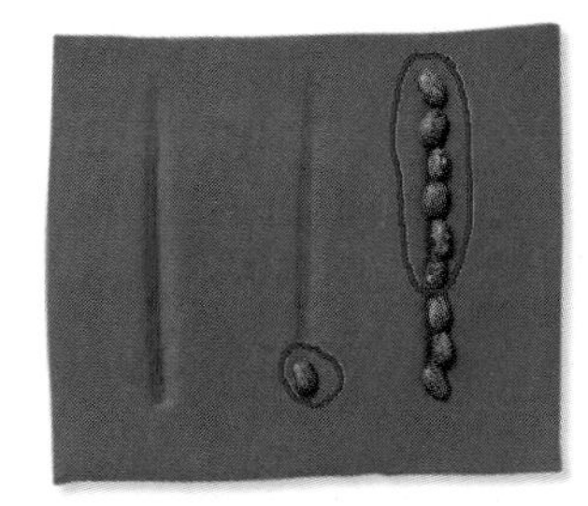

2 Subtract 16 by taking away 6 counters from the ones groove and the counter from the tens groove.

3 The difference is 3.

Glossary

abacus	a frame strung with beads used to do math
abax	a board with grooves and objects, such as pebbles or beans, used to do simple math
counters	pebbles or beans used in a counting board
counting board	a board used in ancient times to do math
frame	something that forms a border or provides support
grooves	long, narrow dents
regrouping	making 10 ones into 1 ten or 1 ten into 10 ones; making 10 tens into 1 hundred or 1 hundred into 10 tens, and so on